SOUTH OF THE *Boredom*

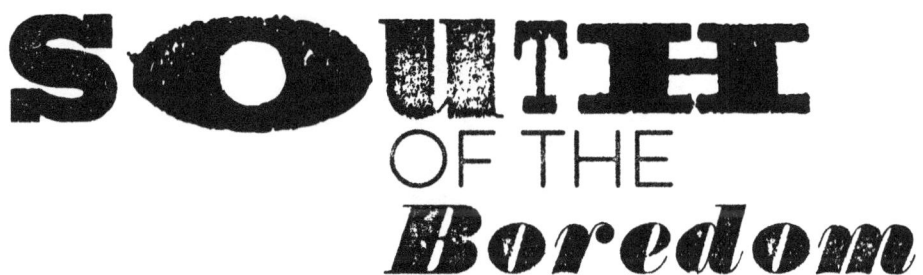

SOUTH OF THE *Boredom*

Jerry Bradley

ANGELINA RIVER PRESS

© 2017 Jerry Bradley
Fort Worth, Texas

Library of Congress Cataloging-in-Publication Data

Bradley, Jerry, 1948 –
    South of the Boredom / Jerry Bradley

    ISBN 978-0-9987364-3-3

    Library of Congress Control Number: 2017960976

Design by Minor Design

Acknowledgments

The author gratefully acknowledges the following publications
where versions of these poems appeared:

CCTE Studies: "Extermination," "El Glóton," "Hecho en Mexico,"
   "Misremembering the Alamo"

Chachalaca Review: "The Chile Fields of Guanajuato," "The Island of the Dolls"

Goodbye, Mexico: Poems of Remembrance: "Boys' Town, Ciudad Acuña,"
   "The Kentucky Club, Juarez," "On the Highway of the Sun"

Helen: "A Brief Glossary of Native Plants"

Main Street Rag: "Chuy Cabra's Taco Truck"

Langdon Review of the Arts: "Cemetery on Isla Mujeres," "Free in the Wild,"
   "Sacrifice at Chichén Itzá," "Train to Copper Canyon," "Undatable"

Parody: "The Deserted Amusement"

Riversedge: "Plaza de la Constitución"

Writing Texas: "Lex et Ordo," "Rubble in San Gervasio," "Xolos outside KFC"

Contents

The Kentucky Club, Juarez	1
Plaza de la Constitución	2
Free in the Wild	3
Train to Copper Canyon	4
Man, Lion, Eagle, Ox	5
Boys Town, Ciudad Acuña	6
Penitentes	8
Funerary Monument in Palenque	9
Perusing the Spanish Dictionary	10
The Island of the Dolls	11
Xolos outside KFC	12
The Lagoon at Xel-Há	13
A Brief Glossay of Native Plants	14
The First Death of Frida Kahlo	15
On the Highway of the Sun	16
Chapulines	18
The Ruins of Tulum	19
Sacrifice at Chichén Itzá	20
Alley of the Kiss	21
Hecho en Mexico	22
The Chile Fields of Guanajuato	23
Feasting in Foreign Lands	24
The Deserted Amusement	25
La Llorona	26
Cemetery on Isla Mujeres	27
Undatable	28
A Mayan Valentine	29
Extermination	30
Los Volodores	31
Fifty Cent Sneakers	32
February Is the Month	33
How an Ant Saved the Aztecs	34
A Caribbean Plunge	35
Lex et Ordo	36
Pueblo Magico	37
The Lords of Poison	38
Before	40
Rubble in San Gervasio	41
Chuy Cabra's Taco Truck	42
The Devil's Alley	43
El Glóton	44
Misremembering the Alamo	45
Pick Up Your Pencils	46

The Kentucky Club, Juarez

the margarita was born
just across the Santa Fe bridge

where Jack Dempsey stumbled out on all fours
where Marilyn celebrated her last divorce
where mescal still masks the thirst of desire

and lust lights their cigarettes

where Chapo moves cocaine
and young soldiers, rifles on their shoulders
languish on the corner

where the jukebox
like the killing never wants to stop

Plaza de la Constitución

The view from the Majestic's roof terrace stuns:
the Zócalo, the Governor's Palace to the east,
the altar of the kings in the cathedral,
the mint, museums, the academy of art.

The constitution was Spain's, not Mexico's,
but every September El Presidente recites the Grito
and pronounces Mexico free again.

It is where Axayácatl and Moctezuma's uncle reigned
and Cortes's palace was built on the bones of Aztec dancers
so every equinox viceroys could be sworn in
despite despots, earthquakes, and floods.

The Olympic marathon began here in '68,
and 18,000 once bared themselves for a camera
near La Santísima, the church of the most holy sacrament,

and during Holy Week from a restaurant
in the Portal de Mercaderes we saw
striking teachers beaten with metal pipes.

Free in the Wild

I emerge from the renovated Playa del Wallet
with all its North American conveniences,
the marina teeming with yachts nearby, too tired
to face another day gazing at eco-park life.

Who wants to see captive stingrays and feel no danger,
much less a glum sanctuaried turtle or reef-diving tourists
beyond the underwater palisade where they churn
amid tons of seaweed floating itself toward shore —
the unavoidable irony of snowbirds watching tropical fish?

Today it's an easy choice: the jungle or drinks at the beach bar
where a sequence of daiquiris under a thatched palapa
may just do the trick. Then to the Blue Parrot's
late-night fire show to see semi-naked dancers twirl
flaming chained batons. Their rear-ends, it is reported,
twitch like the tails of kites. Another attraction not to be missed,
like the rainforest's aviary where on Tuesday we paid to see
creatures (much like these women) once free in the wild.

Train to Copper Canyon

Though it's only four hours on the express,
we want to take the canyon's full measure:
eighty-six tunnels, thirty-seven bridges, fifteen hours,
Guadalajara to the coast (almost) and the Sea of Cortez.

But at Divisadero Barrancas, we have
only fifteen minutes for the locals to sell us
hand-woven baskets and freshly-grilled gorditas.
(How wonderful their caves smell.)

Then back aboard our glass-domed coach, we spot
ringtailed babasuris amid the branches of ironwood
and amapas; overhead micro-hummingbirds, pygmy owls,
and eared quetzals flit, soar, and preen.

The imperial woodpecker and the Mexican wolf
are gone, and the Tarahumara frog is in on the ropes,
but cougars still roam, though they are even shyer
than the bottom-dwelling citizens we meet.

At our next stop a yellow Hummer offers side-trips
to orange groves and farms on the canyon floor where goats,
cattle, and horses range alongside fat Abyssinian burros.
Working sheep dogs vie with unemployed curs for scraps.

It's been quite a trek: pipe-organ cacti, mushrooming boulders,
rock-studded mountain streams that range between emerald hills
and slate-blue lakes. And standing between the cars is like
trying to straddle the Sierra Madre's backbone.

From my window I've seen two gallos fighting over hens
in a barnyard, a fox on the run, a coyote looking for trouble.
No place seems immune from threats. And on a fencepost
a lynx hangs, no longer in possession of its own hide.

Man, Lion, Eagle, Ox

Hovered
above the wreckage
in Coyame where the Cessna fell
onto the greasewood, the seraphs of Ezekiel
wore four faces. Sixteen feet in diameter and five
in height, the disk lay where it collided with the 180, both pilots
as dead as the recovery team from Ojinaga who must have fingered their rosaries
and prayed to the beasts of the gospels, a zodiac of earth, air, fire, and water
(Matthew the lion, Mark the ox, Luke the man, John the eagle)
and picked over the bones as if it were Quetzalcóatl's grave.
Asphyxiation said the bio-chem troops from Ft. Bliss
who hooked a cable to the rubble,

lifted it from the flatbed by Sea Stallion, and then with explosives
destroyed the rest — vehicles, bodies, even the debris itself —
except for those uncashable slivers that sank like Spanish silver at the spot.

South of
the Boredom

Boys' Town, Ciudad Acuña

like the doors at the Palacio de Oro
the women here swing both ways
and gather like schoolgirls
in corner booths to gossip about boys

it's the same at the Durango
where Blandina dispenses her penny-candy besitos
to Texans in stenciled belts
and embroidered shirts

they kiss back, feel her soft chi-chis

for a dollar Adelita would lick the spit
off a dog's lips and for twenty
turn puppy love dog style

but the Extranjero is best for those
on benders, between marriages,
or amid a bad one

pay a boy to watch the car
but keep running money in the trunk
just in case

and when you pull out
drunk but dissatisfied
ignore the Indios
selling chiclets and beads

and the street dogs
that circle the taco cart
like hyenas

convince yourself
you're not one of them,
not just another mongrel
trying to outlast
a bottom-of-the-bottle life

then beat it back to Del Rio
disregarding the fallen night,
the dead dove twisting in your grill

Penitentes

It was the conquistadors who first taught them to suffer.
The Animas, the bent ones, always looking down,
the chains on their ankles rattling as they walk.
The Encruzados stagger like bulls at a carneceria,
trudge the irregular streets stooped from the bundles
of thorns slung across their bare backs. The Flagelantes,
shirtless too, carry rosaries in one hand, whips in the other;
they balance large wooden crosses in the crooks of their arms,
stop at designated times to kneel and flail themselves.

A townsperson playing Judas Iscariot also roams the streets,
his yellow tunic as greasy as his hair. In his hands he jangles
thirty pieces of silver, Taxco silver, straight from the mayor's mines.

Funerary Monument in Palenque

Pakal built the Temple of Inscriptions
in the cedar and sapodilla jungle of the Yucatan
amid toucans and monkeys. His tomb beneath
shows the maize god emerging from the jaws
of the underworld. Above him a celestial bird perches
atop a cross-shaped tree, a snake in its branches.

The living worry about last things, and, like the rest of us,
Pakal lay masked between two worlds with remnants
of human sacrifice all around. He ruled longer
than anyone in the hemisphere, and now he's dead,
buried in the House of Sharpened Spears
with nine warriors to guard his remains.

He wrote glyphs to the gods on the stucco walls
of his own sarcophagus. One panel shows a human figure
in an elaborate feather headdress, jaguar-skin skirt,
beaded cape, and belt. It holds a child, likely Pakal himself.
The children of eternity may live the retired myths
of peacocks, but in death they always roost with serpents.

Perusing the Spanish Dictionary

I started, of course, from the front, the way
beginners do, concentrating upon
the trick of getting each word to resay
itself in an exotic, liquid tongue.
Huichol, nearly midway, referred to those
Indians of the Sierra Madre;
huitlacoche, corn fungus, followed close,
then *javelina*, easier to say,
and other *palabras* like *ruca* (crone),
vato (dude) and sonorous *viaje*.
At *zafacón* (waste basket) I was done
and in failure put the damned thing away,
still lacking the word to name, despite my try,
the widening iris in a lovebird's eye.

The Island of the Dolls

The sons of ancient cultures
take legends seriously, and secretive men
respect simple signs: when an eagle perched
on a cactus in the middle of a dying lake,
the first Aztec souvenir was born.

Escaping Mexico City's sprawl for the afternoon,
we board a non-motorized trajinera and pay the boatmen
to pole us through the Xochimilco canals
where the last reported axolotls live. The craft's
floral arches are as ornate as the gaudy gates of heaven.

Soon a barge of mariachis draws near;
one extends his sombrero for tips,
as an enfilade of vendors speeds
close behind to fox us out of our cash.
Just like the salamanders, we gringos are on our own.

The best-known of the floating chinampas
is Isla de las Muñecas, the Island of the Dolls,
where a loner once fished the body of a drowned girl
from the water. The next day a doll washed up,
and he hung it from a branch. Today

dozens of broken bodies, some decapitated,
others with severed limbs, adorn the trees and fences.
Their soulless eyes are always open, haunt the place;
rumors fly like the whispers of wailing women.
Only the charmed can see the first sign of madness.

Xolos outside KFC

The aroma is about as good
as it can get, and these
Pixar-perfect dogs concur.

Pooches meant to guide
the souls of their owners
after death gather here

to puggle through discarded
cardboard containers
and scrap for fries.

Dogs that once adorned
the tombs of the Toltecs
now defend themselves

from one another
in a near-violent brabble
over skin and backs.

The Aztecs say that man and dog
were made from the same bone,
but today there's little agreement.

After all, they were once
delicacies themselves
reserved for sacrificial ceremonies.

Looking at them, I can't imagine
someone at a funeral or wedding spread
asking *now who here gets the dog*.

The Lagoon at Xel-Há

Protected by the shark fence,
    we enter the brackish water
        in our life-vests and snorkels.

Beneath its surface snapper, spotfins,
    balloonfish, even barracudas laze.
        We watch as turtles and manatees

pass in and out of the underwater grottoes
    like slow spirits easy in the underworld.
        The Maya bus driver says

this is where the waters were born, but bright pericos
    fuss with one another in the branches above
        as if to disagree.

Unlike us the queen conches are protected:
    I am no swimmer, and I know
        the unsmiling surgeonfish

has a row of teeth. So I clasp your ankle,
    my slender lifeline, and hold on as you kick
        us across the lagoon

where, buoyant and resilient with new life,
    I leave it to the parrotfish
        to nibble away my very last sin.

*South of
the Boredom*

A Brief Glossary of Native Plants

Lupine is Latin for bluebonnet; *amargosa*,
feminine for bitter water, is a desert, a bush,
and a ghost town in Nevada's Death Valley.
Mot is a small grove of trees to a Texan
but Irish slang for a girlfriend.

The *mealy-cup sage*, a kind of salvia,
induces visions and affords altered,
sometimes spiritual experiences.
An ox-eye in Europe, the *lazy-daisy*
is just a fancy florist in Beverly Hills.

Which brings us to the *Mexican hat*:
an upright prairie cornflower the Zuni's used
as an emetic when the last traces of an over-
served weekend would not quite quit blooming.

The First Death of Frida Kahlo

Some people are a part of history; others engrave it.

Her right leg shortened by polio, she limped
long before she boarded the bus home.
And when it hit the streetcar — and then a wall —
some died; many were injured. A handrail
pierced her hip, dislocated her feet, shattered
her pelvis and back, left her as broken as Mexico.

World war was coming. Immobilized
in her blue house, she learned to paint:
blood, skulls, even death itself. Alone
she recovered painting the subject she knew best.

Rivera's *Ballad of Revolution* documents
his country's history: in it we see Frida
handing weapons to peasant soldiers,
July 7, 1910, her adopted birthday.

That was before Mexico feared communism,
before he and Frida moved to California —
that sunny image of imperialism she had stood against —
before Trotsky quarreled with Diego
and was ice-axed in his Coyoacán home,
before she left the hospital without her amputated leg.

Her final painting, *Viva la Vida*,
shows sliced red-meated sandias bursting
from their green rinds. Immune
to the baggerment of tyrants, she knew
life was the ribbon tied around the bomb.

*South of
the Boredom*

On the Highway of the Sun

four lanes through the pink mountains
link Acapulco to Mexico City

the most beautiful 165 miles
in Mexico's financial death march

a privatized artery no longer feeding the heart
of machete-wielding peasants
eager to slash coconuts for thirsty travelers

or kids wearing worn-out iguanas
cheap at twice the price

it runs past the Tequesquitengo sugar mill
Cortes built on cane slavery

and the pit where fighting roosters
swear and spit behind the spa's walls
then it's on to Cuernavaca

where Lowry's Consul tried to drink
himself to death in a foothills cantina

to villages where the bedbug hauler
sits throttling his engine

and exhausted men collect
around picnic tables
as evaporative coolers

blow aside dreams as easily
as the aroma of grilled chicken

but if you saw this Mexico
you would understand

why donkey-eared Lampwicks
like us drive on
still yearning for Pleasure Island

and dreaming that Coronado's gold
glistens just beyond
the horizon where even this road ends

*South of
the Boredom*

Chapulines

Early summer and they're everywhere,
browning like tiny lobsters

or being pan-fried to a crisp
with garlic, lime juice, and salt.

At the ballpark
they're toasted with chili.

The soccer team's patch
shows one riding a ball.

Everyone in Oaxaca is eating creatures
who were themselves determined to eat the world.

But I'm as brave as any starving Spaniard —
there's nothing a michelada won't wash down.

The Ruins of Tulum

From the observatory we could see it all:
the only coastal Mayan city, its old city square
with massive castillo, the thick walls
and abandoned watchtowers, its protecting cliffs
from which gods descended into the turquoise Caribbean.

Here Chac, the rain god, still beats the clouds
with snakes and his lightning axe, creates the thunder
that booms loudest on sultry afternoons.

Above the door in the Temple of the Frescoes,
a god with a bird's wings and tail
sits astride a four-legged beast, perhaps a horse,
as it dives into the ocean.

In his graffito (now off limits to tourons)
Estevan brags about sleeping with his brother's wife;
his exaggerated pictogram penis
seems large enough to thrash a donkey.

Sacrifice at Chichén Itzá

After inspecting the altar,
we descend the jaguar walk
away from the red throne

and think of their suffering. Outside
we continue to speak in low voices
even though the slightest whisper

carries all the way to the pyramid's top.
"What about the screams?" we wonder.
Or those who drowned in the sinkhole cenote?

The spring equinox is not really
a season meant for grief, particularly
when we can't tell day from night.

We accept that the sun is dying. But when it
casts its shadow in the last daylight,
a serpent writhes down the darkening steps.

The Alley of the Kiss

I

When two lovers pass through,
they kiss on the third step
to ensure their love lasts.
Hundreds pass through,
counting their steps,
hoping the story is true.

II

Doña Carmen met Don Luis at church
and offered her holy water from his hands.
But her father feared his only daughter
might fall in love with the miner.

He forbade them to speak, sought a better suitor,
but, when Luis passed her house,
he could see her bedroom window could be reached
from the house next door, only a meter apart.

He offered a good price for the house but was denied.
Then he offered his life's savings so that by extending
his hand again he could touch his beloved.
Nothing could discourage him.

That night she found the man of her dreams
inches away from her balcony, close to enough to kiss.
But when her father discovered the couple in an embrace,
he drove a dagger into his daughter's chest.

III

Don Luis held her hand
as a thousand plans turned cold.

Then he threw himself into the mine shaft,
love and death both just one misstep away.

*South of
the Boredom*

Hecho en Mexico

Caught trying to smuggle more than
a hundred dresses back to the States,
two Americanas sit in a holding station,
their fiancés on the other side of the thick glass.

Both men are nearly sober. One, hotter
than a habanero, is freely miserable,
has counted his steps across the narrow room
a dozen times already. They could drive on
without them, but that won't make him happy.
Being bored on alien soil tastes like the slow kiss of death.

It is also Easter, a slow day, and no one
but them is in a hurry. Outside, slow-fingered Federales
search the SUV: glove compartment and console,
spare tire, jack, inside the hubcaps, and under the floors.
Their luggage is piled on the curb.

No one will say how long this may take
or if the sorority back home
will miss out on the latest styles.
It may not be enough today —
though the women are ready to pay a fine
and leave. Instead, without thimbles
they must sew tags of origin in each garment
while they rehearse their stitch-bitch lies.

A mestizo sleeps in the next room. Slumped
in a corner, he snuffles like loud soup
and dreams that zombie Jesus will rise soon
to answer the prayers of the needy —
even when not spoken by a blonde.

The Chile Fields of Guanajuato

Families come from the highlands to the flat farms
to pick tomatillos in Jalisco, bag coffee beans
in Veracruz, and machete cane in Chiapas.

In Baja they de-stem strawberries, but in the chile fields
of Guanajuato children too young to pick
play naked in puddles while babies sleep in the shade of trucks.

Sometimes there are snakes in the rows;
occasionally someone is crushed by a tractor
or pitched from an open bed.

Some drown in irrigation canals or are struck
by disease. The survivors sleep on hard floors, snore,
rule only the abandoned empire of their dreams.

Feasting in Foreign Lands

We start with the rooster water
posing as chicken soup. Then,
forgoing the goat, order
softened fish and the chankings
of an unchewable tuber.

No one here speaks English, but your blouse,
one button open and translucent
in this light, is a revelation promising more.
Then like Eve you order fruit salad
for two, perfecting original sin.

Some disregard what the night promises
and will their bodies to science
as they turn away from the world.
What I want now — and at the end —
is to rise from this table and follow
you inside our squat hotel where
one more time we take off each other's clothes.

The Deserted Amusement

Most things take place
   in the colorless present,
      like standing

interjurisdictional
   between Juarez and El Paso,
      two choices

with a third,
   the dark Rio Grande, just below.
      We spoke promises

on one side,
   hissed denials on the other.
      Still, what we were meant to suffer

we likely already have,
   and our miseries
      have been witnessed

by the vulgar moon
   and the crooked flower
      that call this climate their own.

If one chose according to his need,
   he might not choose at all.
      Rather he might sit

mid-bridge with a margarita
   and a head full of music
      to remind himself

of home,
   of things no longer sung about,
      and life's ever-saddening border.

La Llorona

Cortes's army was plagued by omens:
a serpent woman wandered the great temples
wailing in her undying grief.
Oh, children, where are you?

At curfew the citizens shut themselves
inside their mud homes, and the streets emptied
except for the distressing wails and the white silhouette
they recognized from their windows

hovering above the stony pavement.
She was always gone by the first rays of dawn,
Malinche, the conquistador's mistress
who betrayed her tribe by loving their conqueror.

When asked at the gates of heaven where
her children were, she said she didn't know,
though she had drowned them herself.
Other mothers feared she would take

their firstborn to present to God
as her own. But what else could she do?
When a child drowns, you can't drain the whole river.

Cemetery on Isla Mujeres

"It takes two to make a silence." – Alan Sillitoe

Brought closer by distance, we are about as far east
as we can go, and still everything conspires
to separate us from our vanity. Maybe a painted tomb
at the edge of the sea is all the send-off we should expect.

There are stories here someone should tell, but
reading these stones makes us only more tolerant of death.
And as we walk the narrow rows considering the lives spent,
we wonder what we will live for once our fear at last goes.

The only thing a peso buys anymore is someone
else's thoughts, yet we leave one on an old man's crypt.
Learning to wait like this is an art best practiced by lovers,
and it's far harder than making a young woman cry.

Still, now we know how angry graveyards get when the wind
gets its backbone up, what happens when people try not to forget.

Undatable

Fresh from fields of maize and manioc,
the men of Tabasco dress on Saturdays in white cotton,
each collar accented with a red handkerchief. A broad-brimmed hat
woven from fronds keeps the sun off their flat noses
as, uglier than peccaries, raccoons, and rabbits, they walk
the streets of Villahermosa and drink pulque straight from stoppered bottles.

Their eyes, strabismic and unaligned, follow a woman in a bright rebozo.
When she crosses herself outside the cathedral, their fleshy cheeks puff,
compliment her skirt. The newspaper reports a fatal shooting in a bar.
They study their palms, rub calluses, bare their teeth into a smile,
one that warns how poverty obliterates choice. They shuffle
in their loose shoes, unable to raise their ancient, impassive heads.

A Mayan Valentine

Even in Mexico the gods get envious.
Xochiquetzal was cuter than Cielito Lindo's freckle,
and, when Quetzalcóatl stole the cocoa tree
from paradise, she adorned it with beautiful flowers
and Tlaloc, the god of rain, watered it.

But Tezcatlipoca was jealous and decided
to eradicate cocoa trees from the earth,
so he transformed himself into a pulque seller.
Drink he told Quetzalcóatl. *Lose your troubles.*

He lost his woes — and his celibacy too.
Ashamed and dishonored, Quetzalcóatl vowed
to disappear forever. He picked the last cocoa seeds
as he left, put them in his pocket, and, as he passed
through Tabasco, dropped them into its fertile soil.

Today young swains serenade their amorcitas
in the plaza and offer them balloons and ribbons;
they leave stuffed animals on their doorsteps.
Jewelry and perfume too, cupid figurines —
and of course chocolate. And when nothing else works,
they sprinkle the seeds of their love with Cuervo.

Extermination

Killing off the ants, I think of that vast Yucatan crater
as I shovel deep into the den, my own shockwaves
triggering volcanoes and earthquakes in antdom.

The impact at Chicxulub caused tsunamis —
the largest in history — and for these pests
the hose is next. Some burrow underground;

others run wildly as if this is indeed the end of things.
Dust particles turn to mud. They have
no idea what more may come.

Then when I spread the gasoline and strike,
the match heats them to incandescence, such a fire
as once left even the great dinosaurs staggering.

Los Voladores

You can often catch them, five costumed Aztecs
performing dances atop a tall pole. Their performance is loose:
one plays a flute as others step in a moment's re-creation
of some pre-historic ritual. That's all you need to know.

Many of our own traditions are less imposing,
certainly not so acrobatic. Often off-schedule, we too
work for what amounts to little more than a donation,
and there is always, it seems, someone with a camera
ready to record our failure and banjax the whole shebang.

Our longings carry us only so far;
then we watch for signs, bless ourselves
when they don't come. Having had one chance,
we have little hope for a second as like these flyers
we swing by our heels all the way to the ground.

Fifty Cent Sneakers

A fuerza, ni los zapatos entran.

If you were a cat,
you'd know how to hunt mice.
But if you were a crocodile

like Cipactli, you'd have a jaw
at every joint, eat whatever fell
into the waters of creation,

and squeeze the world to chimbles —
even Tezcatlipoca's foot.
All thirteen heavens were born in her head.

The rest of the universe rode upon her back.
But if you were a cat, your tail
would twitch in the underworld.

You cannot force your shoes to fit —
even though you think you were born
to wear fifty-cent sneakers.

February Is the Month

February is the month
   when little birds match
      and mate.

They dance around each other,
   limb to limb, sing
      one another's merry tune.

But in public parks and small-town squares,
   boys and girls circle each other
      in opposite directions.

On the second pass
   the males offer flowers to the ones
      who have caught their eye.

When Xochipilli, prince of flowers,
   married his twin, a feather
      fell upon her breast,

and she became a luxuriant bird.
   She stuck maguey thorns
      into their tongues

to keep them from begging
   for crumbs during holy fasts.
      Centeotl, god of corn,

was their son. With the promise
   of food or flowers, even
      an old dog may learn to dance.

How an Ant Saved the Aztecs

Before the arrival of the gods,
the Aztecs fed themselves on roots and game.
All the corn lay hidden behind the heart
of massive mountains no one could part.

His priests asked Quetzalcóatl for help,
but not even gods can move mountains.
So he changed into a small black ant
and scaled every fissure and crack.

Months later, behind the tallest peak,
he reached the cornfield and took a grain
back to his people between his teeth.

The Aztecs never knew hunger again.
One kernel brought pastures and farms,
tortillas rounder and yellower than the sun.

A Caribbean Plunge

Parasailing three hundred feet over Nichupte Lagoon,
I can see most of Cancun's fourteen miles of beach
where women in flower necklaces sell curios.
The swells aren't the only shimmer. Wave runners

and banana boats speed by below, and flyriders zip
back and forth like waterbugs in the mangrove channels.
It's not the height I'm afraid of but the depth.
No soup remains hot forever, so what happens

when this ride ends, if I miss the boat
and land amid all this shining sewage?
The wind must hear my knees knocking,
but it's not as loud as the screaming in my head.

Lex et Ordo

The gallero trains his roosters for the Texcoco fair,
cuts away their crests, and injects each cock
with horse steroids, Equipoise, so much
that, when the birds die, they are unfit to eat.

He cleans his best, Jeronimo, to neutralize
the poisons, washes him in salt water,
careful to keep it from his eyes.
Narcos come to these high stakes matches,

men who don't like to lose. The law,
like a dying bird, always looks the wrong way.
But he who has brined a bird has a brother
and a friend; that's what he hears the old men say.

Pueblo Magico

Clustering for warmth like cigarettes in a pack
at ten thousand feet in the oyamel firs,
the monarchs gather in their butterfly biosphere
above Angangueo. Millions have made the migration
from Canada, three thousand miles riding thermals
over mountains and deserts and stuffing
themselves on Midwest milkweed.

Generations were born and died along the way,
the adults living only a few weeks,
but those methuselahs born at summer's end
can outlive snowstorms, mudslides, and floods,
forest fires and illegal deforestation,
tailings that poison the water long after
the mines have folded and springs gone dry.

Home at last, they are like dead souls returning
on Día de los Muertos, troops of unkillable amorists
wearing fragile sugar skulls, so many weary angelitos
puffing together in a crowded ashtray.

The Lords of Poison

Don Fermin was so rich he didn't
have to work, but he always got up early
to pray. And every time he kissed
the feet of Christ, he left a coin in the plate.

Don Ismael was rich too,
but he was envious, spoke ill
of his rival, and cringed
when anyone offered him praise.

In fact Ismael longed to see him dead
and began plotting to murder old Fermin.
He found a curandero with the perfect poison,
a blue liquid that spread slowly through the body.
Don Ismael laced a cake with it
and sent it to Fermin by a mutual friend,
an alderman. Not imagining his danger,
Fermin ate a slice with a steaming cup of chocolate.

Eager to see the results of his crime, Ismael
followed his victim's every step and from a distance
watched every move. And the next morning
he waited for Fermin in church.

When mass ended and Don Fermin knelt
to kiss Christ's feet in prayer,
he barely touched them with his lips
when a dark stain spread across the toes.

Everyone nearby was amazed, but the one
who trembled most was Don Ismael;
he ran to Don Fermín
to confess his guilt

and embraced him in forgiveness
like a lost brother. When news of the miracle
spread through New Spain,
people offered candles and prayed.

Some poisons are like that, painless
and leave no trace, not like when
Fray Diego burned sacred objects
in a bonfire that stayed lit for three days.

Before

Before the Spaniards buried the sun stone
face down outside the viceroy's palace
and Tenochtitlan fell under their rule,

before thousands were sacrificed
beneath the sunken eyes of Tonatiuh,
the fifth sun, the lord of death and flint,

there was the beginning.
Everything was quiet;
there was only sea and sky.

Then the gods decided to create us. First
they tried clay; then they carved wooden idols
who had no understanding of their makers.

So they made us children of corn:
four men and four maidens who learned
to hold each other like husks. Our hair
waved like tassels in the breeze.

Rubble in San Gervasio

Women visit here in tribute to Ixchel,
their goddess of love and fertility. This morning
our tribute costs $4, more if we want photos
or the guided tour. Though the gods won't pay
attention to our prayers, they will press for pesos.

One woman wears an entwined serpent headdress;
crossed bones adorn her skirt. Another grumbles
that the sand makes her feet feel filthy. They want
desire to be delicate, bloom mostly at night,
but this shrine, open only in daytime, closes at 5.

But love teaches that more than feet get dirty,
and here's another reason to be squeamish and wear shoes:
lizards and iguanas, nastier than any penis, wander
the grounds. They are not gods — but they really are something.

Chuy Cabra's Taco Truck

It's just another roachcoach hawking gallina and buche,
its red and green letters proclaiming *locally grown*
with the *cat* in *catering* curiously underscored.
Yet it's hard to know what borders may have been crossed
in these versions of centerline bovine and awesome possum,
flat cat on a tortilla, chargrilled slab of lab, and highway pizza.
Mystery meat to be sure, and anything on the menu might contain
chunk of skunk, smidgen of pigeon, round of hound, smear of deer,
        or rigor mortis tortoise — and Chuy's bumper is banged up pretty bad.

So what if the chili is merely bad-luck buck or too-slow doe?
And what does knowing have to do with what it is — stomach? esophagus? —
or ever was? Goat or goatsucker, have him serve it de chivo or al pastor,
the way the preacher likes them — he'll eat anything in a bun or shell —
and wash it down with a Jarritos or horchata. No sense wasting meat or fowl,
        whether it's snake 'n' bake, German shepherd pie, or even airbrake owl.

Feathers or leathers, varmint or pet,
the slaughterhouse won't toss anything a break,
but there are better ways to go than on a dark farm-to-market
where Chuy's readying to thin the herd.
Savor, while you can, what it is you desire
and wonder, if you must, *"Is that cilantro in the sauce?"*
Then confess to what it is you really fear, just don't ask.
    Would you really prefer poodles with noodles?

The Devil's Alley

Few venture into its dust, particularly
at night when gloom reigns. Some say
even the Devil himself fears it, despite its name.

Still on occasion a brave man ignores
the warnings, and, challenged by friends,
counts his steps to the alley's end.

Clenching his fists, he walks the path
until he feels it begin to give way beneath his feet.
A constable is called who summons a priest

who says — as he always does — "We must placate
the spirit with jewels and coins." The next day
groups of men leave riches as instructed.

"The Devil is nothing more than a thief,
an embezzler," one old fisherman alleges.
"The children of God must be protected."

Then after dark, ready to surprise
that diabolical creature beneath the sand,
he too is struck by a fire in his insides.

He sinks as if he's been smacked from behind.
And indeed he has — but by a lesser devil,
one who wears a collar and carries a poker in his hand.

South of
the Boredom

El Glóton

It's mango season! the supermarket exclaims,
extolling yet another product I seldom eat.
Still I am attracted by the banner's claims

and the offerings from Mexico's monstrous heat:
so many foods endlessly available these days
(even if the color doesn't say much about the meat).

I'm not talking about just fruits and filets,
and who knows when a persimmon is prime
or what rules appetite obeys?

Take the damsons: pricey at any time.
And what the hell is gasper gou
except another fish shiny with mucous and grime

to be rinsed down with a babycham cru?
The wise counterman knows their names,
but for all I know this could be loup garou.

Misremembering the Alamo

Somewhere between Walgreens and the Alamo cenotaph,
spectators gather to witness the replication of the state's
most famous lost cause. The Texians, all old, fire single-shot
rifles toward both ends of the closed street, careful to point away
from vacationers. The Mexicans, uniformed in blue-and-red, fire back.

The cannon they shoot is loud and takes a long time to load.
An hour ago they were hoisting shots with other day-drinkers
inside the Menger. Now between salvos a narrator offers
a small dose of history, but he can't change what's been 180 years
coming. A low-flying drone documents the defeat.
The tallest Texian could probably thwack it with his rifle,
but he acts as if it isn't there, content beguiled by form.

In time the bystanders grow restless, begin to photograph themselves
to prove they were here, eager to be present in someone's life
other than their own. Then suddenly a recording of el degüello blares,
and thirty soldados storm the makeshift barricades.

Their rifles clank, and one by one the old men take a knee
as if this were flag football, and everyone sees what history has become:
something that never happened retold by someone who wasn't there.
A 17-year-old cholo in a wifebeater laughs when the last Texian goes down.

Pick Up Your Pencils

Pick up your pencils, she says,
and we do fearing the future
is in our hands.

In this end-of-year test,
we stare at the pigmented map
of our land, too many states for each

to have its own color,
and pray for names.
I spot Texas, home, right off.

California I know
and penis-shaped Florida.
Between there be dragons.

I have learned to recognize the world's
familiar barriers. East of here
they dredge the intercoastal canal.

Draglines turn like movie monsters
in slow circles
to stalk their prey.

We've heard the warnings:
refugees from Louisiana or worse
are heading this way.

Mexico is due south. There
the sons of garbagemen
play drums.

The Alamo can no longer
keep them back; our pencil boxes
no longer hold everyone's dreams.

About the Author

Jerry Bradley, a member of the Texas Institute of Letters, is University Professor of English and University Teaching Fellow at Lamar University. He is the author of eight books including four poetry collections. In 2017 he won the Boswell Poetry Prize and received creative writing awards from the Conference of College Teachers of English and the Texas College English Association.

Bradley's poems have appeared in *New England Review*, *American Literary Review*, *Modern Poetry Studies*, *Poetry Magazine*, and *Southern Humanities Review*. He is the long-time poetry editor of Concho River Review and is a past-president of the Texas Association of Creative Writing Teachers, the Conference of College Teachers of English, and the Southwest Popular and American Culture Association which endows a writing award in his name.

In 2014 Bradley was named a Piper Professor, an annual award that recognizes ten Texas professors. In 2000 he received the Joe D. Thomas Scholar-Teacher of the Year from the Texas College English Association and the 2005 Frances Hernandez Teacher-Scholar Award given by the Conference of College Teachers of English. He was named Outstanding Alumnus from Midwestern State University's College of Liberal Arts in 2002.

More information is available on his Wikipedia page (Jerry Bradley, poet) and his personal website www.jerrybradley.net.

Crownfeathers and Effigies

Bradley has mastered the kind of poetic voice that is both memorable and unique. ... Bradley somehow captures that place where pain and humor exist together, and he is able to illuminate the imperfect and selfish nature of familial love. ... One of the strengths of Bradley's writing is his straightforward and often unembellished style that has the ability to knock the reader over with simple lines. ... Few books achieve as many quotable moments.

Gretchen Johnson, *Concho River Review*

Bradley wields his exceptional craft to explore how the human heart can repair itself after great loss by wistful and wry reexaminations of the past. ... Bradley gives us narrators who rise from the ashes of relationships and disasters with a renewed sense of self, of the hidden geographies of the heart.

David Bowles, *The Monitor*

The author creates a gendered-male voice that explores the power of persona poetry, interrogating the personal and the universal, mixing them in a way that blurs boundaries between private and planetary tragedies that we all might face. ... This mixture of despair and hope fills these pages in interesting ways, and as readers we're always made privy to the speaker's innermost feelings.

Katherine Hoerth, *Inside Higher Ed*

Bradley tackles complex subjects, oftentimes told with wry humor. The poems have central themes of love, relationships, divorce, history, death, and so forth and are beautifully crafted in an equally beautiful language.

Geosi Gyasi, *Geosi Reads*

Bradley takes our refreshingly sweet mood of yesterday and pokes it full of holes. But I don't mind. The poking is always skillful and frequently sly, the mood leavened with a pleasing black humor at times.

Texas Book Lover

The Importance of Elsewhere

Bradley's form expressively fits its subject ... striking images and sounds ... interwoven rhymes that are worthy of John Keats. ... All of these works illuminate Frost's notion of metaphor, of saying one thing in terms of another. Bradley's handling of figurative language, then, enables him simultaneously to express deep emotion and to do so artfully, not sentimentally.

Matthew Brennan, *American Poetry Review*

In The Importance of Elsewhere Bradley maintains an exemplary standard of literary excellence. His diction is muscular and lean, artfully absent even the slightest hint of carelessness. Whether working in free verse or executing the rigorous demands of the sonnet or rhymed triplet, Bradley writes with the consummate poetic skill of a master.

Larry D. Thomas, Texas Poet Laureate 2008

Daring but mature talent that new poets could study with benefit and seasoned poets will undoubtedly admire. ... Bradley refuses to dodge the hard questions, to make them other than they are ... his strong gift for metaphor. ... Jerry Bradley is one of our state treasures.

Jan Seale, *Texas Books in Review*

Bradley is an exceptionally fine poet whose major fault as a poet is that he waits too long between books ... beautifully written and poignant. ... Bradley's poetry twists and turns on a sharp pinprick of wit that lifts it from the everyday personal poetry we have become accustomed to ... filled with moments of grace ... a book that rewards many readings for its wit, its compassion, its basic honesty, but mostly because of the poet's firm control of language and the basic, down to earth, rightness of the poems.

Palmer Hall, *Yanaguana Literary Review*

Bradley moves seamlessly between nostalgia, humor, hope, and sorrow ... the beauty and pain of daily life ... he pushes us to see simple truths.

John Wegner, *Concho River Review*

Highly recommended for poetry lovers and libraries.

Janet Turk, *Review of Texas Books*

Simple Versions of Disaster

Powerful and haunting poems.

Books of the Southwest

Bradley's poetry implies that artistic creation is redemptive for the artist, including the poet, and an inspiration for us all.

Betsy Colquitt, *Texas Books in Review*

Jerry Bradley's poems seem to give up their message readily to the reader, but then they keep ringing with the grace of their style and the ripples of their meanings. I think Bradley should be recognized as one of the charter members of the New Clarity School of Poetry.

Richard Sale, *University of North Texas Press*

What is contained in this delightful collection of poetic observations is ... a remarkable wisdom that emerges from experiencing the disasters of everyday life.

Clay Reynolds, *Fort Worth Star-Telegram*

A volume of poetry that hits the eye with a fresh view of life that even a poetry hater can love. ... This book is a fine example of what purpose contemporary poetry must have, a relevancy to modern life.

Texas Writer's Newsletter

I like the wit, toughness, sensitivity, and complexity.

Dick Heaberlin, *Western American Literature*

An interesting range of formal strategies, from open-form stanzas to cinquains and sonnets.

R. S. Gwynn, *Review of Texas Books*

How breathlessly this poet speaks. ... Lines of uncommon pungency jump out at the reader, forcing the reader to re-read their contexts. ... This is mighty fine writing.

David Castleman, *Dusty Dog Reviews*

Other Books by Jerry Bradley

Poetry

Crownfeathers and Effigies, Lamar University Literary Press

The Importance of Elsewhere, Ink Brush Press

Simple Versions of Disaster, University of North Texas Press

The Great American Wise Ass Poetry Anthology (with Ulf Kirchdorfer), Lamar University Literary Press

Criticism

The Movement: British Writers of the 1950s, Twayne Publishers

Famous American Writers (with Samio Watanabe and Jerry Craven), Asahi Press

Famous British Writers (with Samio Watanabe and Jerry Craven), Asahi Press

www.ingramcontent.com/pod-product-compliance
Lightning Source LLC
Chambersburg PA
CBHW020959090426
42736CB00010B/1392